HEAL YOUR LIFE WORKBOOK

RESOURCES AND TOOLS FOR CLEARING EMOTIONAL BAGGAGE SO YOU CAN LOVE YOUR LIFE

SHARON WHITEWOOD

BALBOA.
PRESS

A DIVISION OF HAY HOUSE

Balboa Press books may be ordered through booksellers or by contacting:

Balboa Press
A Division of Hay House
1663 Liberty Drive
Bloomington, IN 47403
www.balboapress.com.au
1 (877) 407-4847

ISBN: 978-1-4525-2556-3 (sc)
ISBN: 978-1-4525-2557-0 (e)

Printed in the United States of America.

Balboa Press rev. date: 09/08/2014

Contents

Acknowledgements

As always with any written work, many people have influenced, contributed to and directly informed the work. This workbook is no different.

My particular thanks go to those who in following their intuitions, ideas and paths have developed these techniques. Their groundwork has already made a huge difference in many lives.

Dr Roger Callaghan whose development of the Tapping protocols has created an amazing tool that has helped many.

Gary Craig who in refining Roger Callaghan's work into the Emotional Freedom Technique has created a technique both delightfully simple yet profound in effect. His generosity in making it freely available to people as well as creating fabulous teaching tools with his video series, has generated a profound movement in healing.

Gene Gendlin who in developing the Focusing process provided a means for people to find their own truth by tuning into their 'felt' sense and body wisdom.

To the many writers who provided guidance on the journaling process; Tristine Rainer, Ira Progoff and Kay Leigh Hagan.

I also thank my friends Karen Dawson and Katie Bestevaar for their reading of the manuscript, suggestions and most of all their positive feedback and encouragement through the challenges of writing and publishing.

To all my teachers with gratitude and love

Introduction

I have written this workbook for a simple reason. I want others to have access to these wonderful resources so they can do their own inner work to heal their hearts and live life to the fullest.

Many people don't have access to counselling support due to remote location, costs and/or painful histories with the 'helping' professions. Many will have the capacity to manage their own development and practice, and so can use these tools to develop their self-awareness, capacity to learn and release painful experiences.

This workbook is also for people who want to work independently, and experience the sense of achievement in personal growth and emotional healing. Too many of us have lost confidence in our own *knowing*, and become dependent on professionals' interpretation.

Depending on your own capacity and confidence, you may find it beneficial to develop a professional relationship to support your inner work, while continuing to use these skills and ideas by yourself.

True healing requires discipline and commitment either way.

These are resources and exercises that support your ongoing self-discovery and self-healing. Ultimately we must heal ourselves from the inside out; others may help, support and guide us but for true healing to occur we must take responsibility for our own emotions, bodies and minds.

If we do not heal from within, any physical or emotional improvements will most likely be temporary. Others may give us nutritional supplements or drugs, massage or Reiki treatments or help us work through the pain of the past. Only we can use discipline to practice a life that is healing and integrated of our minds and being. Deep changes happen, when we open ourselves and let go.

We are responsible. We choose or not. It is a journey of healing, growth and self-realisation. No one else can live it for you or tell you how to live it. There is no owner's manual for operating this being that is you.

We live in a time of human history when there are more choices than ever before. Our parents and their parents did not have the choices we have today and may have become stuck in predictable patterns of living. We do have those choices when we seek out knowledge and apply it to ourselves and our life choices.

Though it is not always an easy choice, it is a great joy to live fully in each moment as we create ourselves anew.

Welcome to the journey of healing yourself.

Chapter 1

SETTING THE CONTEXT

Over the last couple of decades, through my own need for healing, I have found several tools and skills that I have used consistently to heal emotionally from childhood trauma and inadequate care. These techniques and processes, have helped me become aware of who I am, and to make better choices for myself.

This is the knowledge I want to share with you. You may have come to this book with a clear purpose in mind or as a result of confusion and distress. However your reaching for this material has come about, it was most likely driven by an inner prompting, a need or pain, that so disturbs you that you must find a way to feel better.

There are two key ideas that can *enable* us even in that distress; the first is that pain is a driver and without it most of us would not shift in our behaviour and attitudes. The second is that our feelings are vital signals to action and living our truth.

That may seem self-evident. However, our society, family and workplace cultures often encourage us to deny our feelings, and work only with analysis and decisions. We are pushed to *do* and *act* rather than *reflect* and *feel*. Yet painful feelings, denied experiences have to go somewhere in our systems, and so often end up as pain, and finally even disease in our physical bodies, which we endeavour to medicate away.

Paying attention to our feelings takes time, becoming aware of intuitions and insights takes reflection, and allowing images and feelings to come into our awareness, takes openness and trust. We have to go more slowly and tune into ourselves constantly.

Awareness takes time and discipline, a willingness to 'not know' and allowing the knowing to arise in us. Our technological and city-based living encourages us to go faster and do more and more; yet we often gain limited satisfaction in this, but end up feeling more and more disconnected from ourselves, our families and mates. We may also feel disconnected from our communities and from nature.

Not surprisingly our happiness arises from inside of us. It is a naturally occurring feeling that also gets suppressed, when we deny our other feelings. When we do this the painful feelings build up and often burst forth, sometimes inappropriately.

A key message is this. Your feelings are real and important and need to be fully felt and experienced to experience life and move on.

We often spend lots of time and money trying to understand *why* we feel as we do, but understanding rarely resolves and releases pain.

A Unique Time in Human Evolution

We human beings are unusual in the animal world, in that we are born with a limited number of instinctive behaviours, such as the flight or fight mechanism.

Instead, we have a huge capacity for learning behaviour, skills and tools, and the way we learn these, is through watching others do things successfully and through making mistakes. Mistakes create emotional pain which is a deterrent to doing a 'wrong' thing again. The term 'wrong' becomes emotionally loaded with feelings of judgement, guilt and shame.

Many parents in their efforts to teach children and young adults how to live in the world use fear and guilt and shame as penalties. When this happens *constantly*, the mistakes that we make in order to learn, can become deep wounds, loaded with these feelings. These wounds are formative and often *transformative* in our lives. However, the down side is that we often carry these wounds with all of their pain, as if they were all that we are and can be; often we don't learn the real lesson.

Let me make explore that further with you.

Seeing yourself only as *wounded* is not transformative. There is no learning in it and it becomes the only thing you can offer to others; saying this is who I am. This is often what creates and sustains co-dependent relationships; you have your pain and I have mine. It also says "I come to you in hope of healing, but I cannot let go of my pain".

What is needed is to feel it fully and release it.

Wounds not fully experienced and felt create emotional and even physical ill health. They are dysfunctional and debilitating for our lives and everyone we come in contact with. In my country Australia, we say "so-and-so has a chip on his shoulder", an attitude of pain and suffering he or she is carrying around, an anger through which he or she see the world and every experience. Often, something has happened that has caused this pain or fear and the person is still living through that.

Having spent most of my life stuck in such a process I do not judge others only encourage the development of awareness, healing processes and release of pain.

One of the problems for the human species, is that what parents teach children of their own experience and learning, becomes quickly outdated in our fast-moving world. As a consequence, those teachings are based on ways of thinking and feeling that have largely lost their relevance and functionality. This learning or accepted knowledge can often become prejudice and fear-based functioning.

It also becomes the lens that limits what we see in the world, and in ourselves, and therefore limits our behavioural choices. When we share with children, the *reality* of what we have experienced through stories and the telling of that experience directly, they are better able to choose what this experience means for themselves, uncluttered with others' fear, pain and prejudice.

Children and adults love to hear stories. Why is that? Is it an in-built instinct or mechanism for the transfer of experience and learning? What we dislike is the didactic and the directive; because we are by nature primed for exploration and learning.

What I want to highlight here is that there are depths to our being that direct our behaviour and thinking and feeling that we must explore in order to really change.

OVERVIEW OF TECHNIQUES

Over many years I have found specific skills and practices essential for learning about inner processes, changing behaviour in a deep way and in releasing old patterns. In combination, these have transformed my process of healing.

If you have been reading self-development books, going to seminars, and are still feeling frustrated with a lack of progress, it may well be due to some missing skills. Those skills that enable the application and integration of your learning.

The techniques I am referring to, are simple and available. You may have heard of all of them and have used some of them. However, it is the combination and application of them that provides the leverage in shifting blocks and moving through issues more effectively.

The techniques are;

- journaling
- focusing
- emotional freedom technique

These three techniques are *processes* for reflection, unpacking and releasing past and current issues.

While these techniques are simple in concept, we are dealing with the most complex system in the world, the human being. When you are working from inside out, with all of the subjectivity and complexity of the human psyche, the process is even more challenging.

These skills underpin the development process and the cycle we typically go through to learn. Some of us will have learned these skills as we grew up but most won't.

As well as explaining these skills and how to develop and apply them, I also want to give you some self-development maps and models. Although they are just ways of thinking about how we function, and are not 'the truth' or the only way, they are helpful. I am not sure where the saying came from but it is relevant to this process.

"The map is not the territory"

Models and maps can both expand and limit our thinking and that is one of the things we need to challenge when learning. Albert Einstein, a famous and highly successful thinker and scientist is quoted as saying;

"We can't solve problems by using the same kind of thinking we used when we created them."

So when we come to deal with our accumulated knowing, behaviour and attitudes, it is necessary to develop different ways of thinking about ourselves and how we function in the world.

For instance, if someone identified that he had become too negative and judgemental, part of his first stage of changing this, would involve learning both *how he was currently negative and how positive thinking would look, sound and feel different.* Otherwise he will spend unnecessary time beating himself up for being negative because that is how he currently operates.

One of the prime issues for self-development is that when people begin to learn a new skill, they often don't give themselves adequate time to learn. It take six months to fully integrate any new skill or behaviour.

We sometimes have unrealistic expectations of ourselves and *while we understand something with our minds, applying and developing of the skill requires consistent effort.*

This book isn't about a single simple answer. We are profoundly complex beings, and learning arises from reflection on past and current issues, the practice of skills, absorbing new ideas, and being stimulated and challenged.

You will find as you begin learning these skills, that one in particular will be more central to your development process. The other skills will become integrated through that core skill. At this point however, let us get on with identifying and learning these skills.

Journaling, focusing, and EFT or Meridian Tapping are all skills for developing, healing and recreating the inner self. They are the means of bringing forth into our awareness the thoughts, images, words and feelings we experience everyday so we can choose to keep or change them.

They are essential skills to reflecting on our experience and the resultant thinking and functioning, that may need to change.

They also enable us to release emotions, find the silent space of the spirit and integrate ourselves. We often live our lives in compartments and roles, and this can lead to a sense of disjointedness and emptiness. In addition the consumer society promotes the pursuit of material satisfactions and this means living in the outer world.

We cannot live like this. We are organic and complex beings and need to find our inner path to live sustainably.

DEFINITIONS

Journaling is the practice of setting down in words and/or pictures on paper on an on-going basis reflections on daily events, expression of clouded or overwhelming feelings, dream analysis, visualisation results, meditation peaks & troughs, choices, life history review, inner prompting, and inner dialogues. *The journal has always been considered a great way to see the repeating patterns of our behaviour, thinking and feeling, and these are the clues to the inner experience and unconscious triggers.*

Focusing is the practice of becoming aware of your body wisdom and the inbuilt felt senses so you can engage with and release emotions and pain. It is a gentle placing of awareness and attention into the body and respecting the feelings as messages from your body wisdom. *Major shifts in functioning, better decision-making and integration of different voices into your life processes are available through this process.*

Emotional Freedom Technique or Meridian Tapping is a tapping protocol on specific acupuncture Meridian end points to remove the emotional charge from painful past experiences and traumas. These experiences are the underpinning drivers and triggers for dysfunctional behaviour and reactions to life events.

EFT is being used by practitioners and individuals across the world for childhood abuse, sexual and war traumas, anxiety and depression, as well as many physical symptoms.

Clearly there is more to all of these techniques, and I will explore them in detail in the following chapters, and provide clear instructions on developing the skills.

SPIRITUAL PATHS AND AWARENESS

Many people who are oriented to spiritual practice or the New Age movement, enjoy and value on guided meditations, astral travel, essential oils, crystals and Angelic card readings. These activities are uplifting, inspiring, fun and healing.

However, it is important to balance these with clearing of blocks, attitudes and conflicted thinking, so that the deep connection to spirit is made possible. It is the work *within* that makes the richness of humanity and spirituality available and an ongoing presence in each life.

> *"One does not become enlightened by imagining figures of light,*
> *but by making the darkness conscious."* **(C.G. Jung)**

It is vital to maintain the disciplines of journaling, focusing and EFT to fully open the self to the spiritual experience.

Balancing the inner *work* with the satisfactions of treatments, group activities and fun is the key.

SOME CAUTIONS IN USING THESE TECHNIQUES

My experience has been that our psyches normally offer up our issues and blocks at a rate we can cope with. However, while you are learning these skills and doing your inner work, this can occasionally feel overwhelming.

I do recommend that you find a counsellor or friend with more experience to help you when you need it. It might be inner work but it is common to all of us, so seek help and take care of yourself.

Please check out the Maps and models chapter for a **psychological framework** to be aware of in your own process and learning.

Chapter 2

BEGINNING TO LEARN TECHNIQUES

These techniques will help you to reflect on, and release your emotional baggage. Practicing them builds your personal skills in managing problems and developing your resilience.

Reflection is a key step in learning and letting go, one not highly encouraged in our current fast-paced society, but one absolutely necessary to healing.

Reviewing and reflecting on your experience, allows you to see choices where you might usually assume none. Many choices we make automatically, are actually not healthy as they are based on family programming and our own negative experiences. So reflection is the first step to making better choices.

Check out the learning cycle and learning style maps in Chapter 7 on Maps and Models.

So some of these techniques will suit you well and others may be a struggle to persist with. Do learn each one and use it as they work well together. Sometimes exploring your experience and feelings through a different mechanism can provide greater insight.

It is important that you develop some confidence in each technique and process before moving on to learn the next one.

There is a chapter providing exercises for integration later on. This will help you consolidate your use of the combined techniques.

You will get better results in releasing emotional baggage and learning the techniques if you take it slowly. If you try to rush through and apply the techniques too quickly, the process could become frustrating and you may find it difficult to persist.

Chapter 3

JOURNALING

Journal Therapy is a healing process allowing the writer to improve physical, spiritual, and emotional wellness, through the processing of events and emotions, and the creation of new meaning out of these experiences.

Unlike traditional diary writing, where daily events and external happenings are recorded, Journal Therapy focuses on the writer's internal experiences, reactions, and perceptions. Through this process, the writer is able to perceive their experiences more clearly, which has been shown to have both mental and physical health benefits.

There is scientific evidence that the benefits of writing out inner turmoil are more than just psychological. Dr. James Pennebaker, a researcher in Texas, has conducted studies that show that when people write about emotionally difficult events or feelings for just 20 minutes at a time over three or four days, their immune system functioning increases.

Journal Therapy has been used effectively for grief and loss, coping with life-threatening or chronic illness, recovery from addictions, eating disorders and trauma, repairing troubled relationships, increasing communication skills, developing healthier self-esteem, gaining a new perspective on life and clarifying life goals.

Journal therapy is also very effective in groups, and it is common for group members to establish a deep sense of connection as authentic self-expression is shared.

See more at: http://www.goodtherapy.com.au/flex/journal

> **Pick up a pen and a spiral bound writing pad and write.**
>
> What do you feel? Right now?
>
> What has happened to you today that triggered pain from past experiences?
>
> What feelings are arising in you related to an event coming up this weekend?
>
> When we allow our minds to run their patterns of criticism and judgement without getting them out, we are tend to remain under the control of these processes.
>
> Writing down what is running through your mind enables you to get beyond that mental and emotional routine, and allows other feelings, memories and insights to arise. These can tell us something completely different about what is happening to us and why.
>
> *For example, if feeling low or sad, writing about that and what is in awareness enables another layer of awareness to come through, maybe feelings of being imprisoned by a work environment or family or your own expectations.*
>
> *Explore what these feelings are related to, when the situation was first experienced, tease out the place, time and players; can you see some different ways of judging this experience? What might those other people have thought about that experience?*

You could start your journal even with what you "feel" about journaling. This is a vital dialogue with yourself and at a deeper level then your normal awareness. There are many books and websites on Journaling, but it really is about what works for you.

I have had people say to me that they never knew how they really felt about themselves and their life until they started writing.

Journaling enables you to access different levels of your being and feeling. It is your space to express yourself unfettered by other's expectations and needs. It is your private space where you respect and accept your feelings and thinking and explore what effects these have on your life. Many people only become aware of how negative their mental loops are, when they start to record them.

Some simple guidelines will help you set reasonable boundaries.

> ***Don't allow others involved or otherwise to read unresolved issues***; you are at your most vulnerable and need to work through issues for yourself. By all means work with a Counsellor and allow them to read your journal, but you need to feel entirely safe and secure in being completely honest for yourself. Whatever makes you feel unsafe is *not* ok.
>
> ***Write regularly, preferably daily***; you will develop your self-awareness and skills in reflection more quickly if disciplined about your writing exercise.
>
> ***Listen deeply for your thoughts and feelings and ask yourself questions*** starting with "How or what" rather than why. How do I feel, or what has happened? The word 'Why' tends to put us into a rationalising mentality and can create a sense of defending our actions or responses. None of which is at all useful in gaining awareness or self-insight.

There are specific exercises for you to do at the end of this chapter, but if you always start your journal entry with "I feel....." you will be on the right track.

Journaling can be about every area of your life from family relations, health issues, past abuse or trauma experience, partners, work issues, community activities and your spiritual life.

At its simplest using a journal to download the activities of the day, means that they don't continue to run through your mind when you are ready to go to sleep.

The key result from using a journal effectively is increased self-awareness and release of day-to-day pressures. It is a great self-development tool as being aware of your thinking, feeling and functioning is the first step to choosing differently.

Journals have been used for a great variety of purposes from official to political, pillow talk to deep psychological analysis. Ira Progoff developed a journaling system called the Intensive Journal dividing different aspects of individual experience into different parts of a journal. You can search on the internet for further information about this method.

I suggest that you read widely in the field of self-development so as to stimulate your thinking and feeling.

The examples below do not use the true names of people.

Examples

1. Jo had high levels of anxiety and feelings of being socially excluded over many years. She had a husband and three children under 8 years old and really couldn't 'connect' with her peers. She was highly self-critical. There was always something to do and she was endeavouring to give her family homemade breads, vegetarian meals and maintain a house, vegetable plot and extensive garden without much help from her husband.
    She reported finding the journaling process very useful in helping her release her daily frustration and in becoming more aware of the thinking-feeling patterns that generated her anxiety. It was her time for herself and a way of appreciating and teasing out her own unique experiences.

2. Meryl really struggled with journaling as she couldn't find the words to express how she felt. She could write about what had happened during the day but her *feeling* responses were much more difficult to give words to. We worked on building her vocabulary by going through her journal and discussing where the *feelings* were in her body and finding words that expressed 'tension', anxiety/fear and other feelings. Over time she was able to be more articulate about her experiences and separate these from who she was. She became less overwhelmed and driven by these.

Exercises

1. Take out your journal and pen/pencil and doodle a long looping line across the first page. Choosing 3 points along that line (no rules) write a word or phrase that feels right for that point. Be playful and relaxed – wait for a word or two to just arise from your mind. Take one of those word points and write a small story about it as if you were telling it to a child.

    Now ask yourself inside 'what does this mean to me?' Don't be concerned if something doesn't come up immediately or if there is a sudden flood of thoughts. Just note the key words and ideas that speak to you.

    This exercise may set you off on a long journal entry – just go with the flow……

    It may also provide nothing obvious immediately but something may come to mind the next day – note this in your journal when it does.

    The idea is to start to open up to your experience and some of the underlying unconscious patterns. Just be aware of this as a journey of opening yourself up.

2. Think about one of your parents and write a description of them as a parent and a person. How did/do you see them and what might others say?

    What events/ experiences influenced your perception of them?

    How are you like them? Is this something you appreciate or not? What do you do differently?

3. What has been an important event in your life? In what way did this experience change you and what did you learn from it?

    How has it influenced your life? How has it contributed to the story that you tell about your life?

4. Think about a day in the last few months when you took time out for yourself. What were the circumstances and what did that time out do for you? Describe yourself before and after.

Your reflections

This space is for you to reflect on the ideas presented, examples and exercises – what has been useful? What have you learned about yourself? You may transfer these to your journal to further tease out the ideas and reflections.

. . . .
. . . .
. . . .
. . . .
. . . .
. . . .
. . . .
. . . .
. . . .
. . . .
. . . .
. . . .
. . . .
. . . .
. . . .
. . . .
. . . .
. . . .
. . . .
. . . .
. . . .
. . . .
. . . .
. . . .
. . . .
. . . .
. . . .
. . . .
. . . .

Chapter 4

FOCUSING

Focusing is a term used specifically by Eugene Gendlin, to describe a process for gaining access to your inner felt senses and body wisdom.

It is hard for us sometimes to know how we feel, when so many 'shoulds' bombard us. The expectations of others and our own often distract us from our own needs and desires.

Focusing as a daily part of life and awareness, enables a kind of checking in and allowing whatever feelings are in your body, to be *in awareness* and to enable their messages to become part of any decision-making and direction. They tell a truth that is unique to each of us, that cannot be rationalised away or dismissed.

Using *Focusing* enables you to bring physical sensations into your awareness, to be present and connected to these inner feelings, and to learn to trust those senses for their own unique truth.

Focusing is a body-oriented process of self-awareness and emotional healing.

It's as simple as noticing how you feel, and then having a conversation with your feelings in which *you* do most of the listening. Focusing starts with the familiar experience of feeling something in your body that is about what is going on in your life.

When you feel jittery in your stomach as you stand up to speak, or when you feel tightness in your chest as you anticipate making a crucial phone call, you are experiencing what we call a "felt sense", a body sensation that is meaningful.

So what do you do when you have a jittery feeling or tightness or choking sensation in your throat? If you are like most of us, you try to get rid of it. Maybe you curse it a little: "Why does this stupid feeling have to come now, just when I need to be my best?" Or maybe you put yourself down: "If I were a better person, I wouldn't freeze up this way". Maybe you do deep breathing exercises, or have a drink or a cigarette.

What doesn't occur to you, unless you know Focusing, is to listen to the feeling, to let it speak to you.

And yet, when you let the feeling speak to you, you are allowing yourself to be more open to the depth and richness of your whole self. Furthermore, when you listen to the feeling, it is much more likely to relax, release, and let you go on with what you're doing in a clear and centred way. You might even move forward in this area of your life in ways that surprise and delight you.

Focusing is the process of listening to your body in a gentle, accepting way and hearing the messages that your inner self is sending you. It's a process of honouring the wisdom that you have inside you, becoming aware of the subtle level of knowing that speaks to you through your body.

The results of listening to your body are insight, physical release and positive life change. You understand yourself better, you feel better and you act in ways that are more likely to create the life you want.

Focusing begins with bringing awareness into the body, especially the throat, chest, stomach and abdomen.

We don't try to find a feeling, or try to *make* something happen, but we invite something to be felt by asking a gentle open question such as *"What wants my awareness now?"*

When we first find a feeling, we acknowledge it by saying an inner hello to it, and then we describe or name it.

In the next stage of Focusing, we sit down with the feeling to get to know it better, with an attitude of interested curiosity.

We take time to allow a little more meaning to come from the feeling, perhaps a word for an emotional quality. Then we check the word with the feeling, to make sure it feels right.

We are not in a hurry. We create an inner atmosphere of no pressure, just being with what's there. We ask gentle questions as a way of inviting the feeling to tell us more.

In Focusing, change comes in steps, small (usually) realisations, each one of which feels right and makes some difference in the body. After each one, we could stop and focus again another time, or we could keep going, perhaps with another gentle question.

The meaning that is in the body is sometimes connected with a memory, a belief or attitude, or an unmet need or an unexpressed part of ourselves. There is no need to 'fix' or 'solve' the problem. Acknowledging the message, really hearing it, is all that is needed to bring deep relief.

Ending a Focusing session happens slowly and respectfully. We may want to stay for a while with good feelings. We thank the body and say we'll be back.

Life circumstances may bring back feelings that were there in the Focusing session. This is an opportunity for 'mini-focusing' – a little bit of Focusing in the midst of life.

Focusing is a process of listening to something inside you that wants to communicate with you. And yet, like a shy animal, it may first need to discover that you are trustworthy, and that you have created a safe place for it, before it can deliver its message.

- Being in a relationship with your feelings
- Being a good listener to yourself
- Being a friend to your felt sense
- When you are not feeling friendly then deal with that
- Hearing all voices
- The wisdom of not knowing
- Following the felt sense
- Every focusing session is unique

What follows is a lightly edited excerpt from The Focusing Manual, chapter four of *Focusing*.

"The inner act of focusing can be broken down into six main sub-acts or movements. As you gain more practice, you won't need to think of these as six separate parts of the process. To think of them as separate movements makes this process seem more mechanical than it is, or will be, for you, later. I have subdivided the process in this way because I've learned from years of experimenting that this is one of the effective ways to teach focusing to people who have never tried it before.

Think of this as only the basics. As you progress and learn more about focusing you will add to these basic instructions, clarify them, and approach them from other angles. Eventually, perhaps not the first time you go through it, you will have the experience of something shifting inside.

So here are the focusing instructions in brief form, manual style. If you want to try them out, do so easily, gently. If you find difficulty in one step or another, don't push too hard, just move on to the next one. You can always come back. (The following could be recorded)

Clearing a space

What I will ask you to do… will to be silent, just to be quiet and still in yourself. Take a moment just to relax . . .

All right – now, inside you, I would like you to pay attention inwardly, in your body, perhaps in your stomach or chest.

Now see what comes *there* when you ask, "How is my life going? What is the main thing for me right now?"

Sense within your body, let the answers come slowly from this sensing. When some concern comes, DO NOT GO INSIDE IT. Stand back and say "Yes, that's there. I can feel that, there."

Let there be a little space between you and that. Then ask what else you feel. Wait again, and sense. Usually there are several things.

Felt Sense

From among what came, select one personal problem to focus on.

DO NOT GO INSIDE IT. Stand back from it.

Of course, there are many parts to that one thing you are thinking about, too many to think of each one alone. But you can *feel* all of these things together.

Pay attention there where you usually feel things, and in there you can get a sense of what *all of the problem* feels like. Let yourself feel the unclear sense of *all of that*.

Handle

What is the quality of this unclear felt sense? Let a word, a phrase, or an image come up from the felt sense itself.

It might be a *quality* word, like *tight, sticky, scary, stuck, heavy, jumpy* or a phrase, or an image. Stay with the quality of the felt sense till something fits it just right.

Resonating

Go back and forth between the felt sense and the word (phrase, or image). Check how they resonate with each other.

See if there is a little bodily signal that lets you know there is a fit. To do it, you have to have the felt sense there again, as well as the word.

Let the felt sense change, if it does, and also the word or picture, until they feel just right in capturing the quality of the felt sense.

Asking

Now ask: what is it, about this whole problem that makes this quality (which you have just named or pictured)?

Make sure the quality is sensed again, freshly, vividly (not just remembered from before). When it is here again, tap it, touch it, be with it, asking, "What makes the whole problem so _____?" Or you ask, "What is in *this* sense?"

If you get a quick answer without a shift in the felt sense, just let that kind of answer go by. Return your attention to your body and freshly find the felt sense again. Then ask it again.

Be with the felt sense till something comes along with a shift, a slight "give" or release.

Receiving

Receive whatever comes with a shift in a friendly way. Stay with it a while, even if it is only a slight release.

Whatever comes, this is only one shift; there will be others.

You will probably continue after a little while, but stay here for a few moments.

IF DURING THESE INSTRUCTIONS SOMEWHERE YOU HAVE SPENT A LITTLE WHILE SENSING AND TOUCHING AN UNCLEAR HOLISTIC BODY SENSE OF THIS PROBLEM, THEN YOU HAVE FOCUSED.

It doesn't matter whether the body-shift came or not. It comes on its own. We don't control that."

This is an excerpt from the audiotape called <u>Introduction to Focusing</u>, by Ann Weiser Cornell, available from <u>Focusing Resources</u>, 2625 Alcatraz Avenue, #202, Berkeley CA 94705-2702.

Imagine being on the phone with someone you love who is far away, and you really miss that person, and you just found out in this phone call that you're not going to be seeing them soon. You get off the phone, and you feel a heaviness in your chest, perhaps around the heart area.

Or let's say you're sitting in a room full of people and each person is going to take a turn to speak, and as the turn comes closer and closer to you, you feel a tightness in your stomach, like a spring winding tighter and tighter.

Or let's say you're taking a walk on a beautiful fresh morning, just after a rain, and you come over a hill, and there in the air in front of you is a perfect rainbow, both sides touching the ground, and as you stand there and gaze at it you feel your chest welling up with an expansive, flowing, warm feeling. These are all felt senses.

If you're operating purely with emotions, then fear is fear. It's just fear, no more.

But if you're operating on the felt sense level, you can sense that *this* fear, the one you're feeling right now, is different from the fear you felt yesterday.

Maybe yesterday's fear was like a cold rock in the stomach, and today's fear is like a pulling back, withdrawing. As you stay with today's fear, you start to sense something like a shy creature pulled back into a cave.

You get the feeling that if you sit with it long enough, you might even find out the real reason that it is so scared. A felt sense is often subtle and as you pay attention to it you discover that it is intricate. It has more to it. We have a vocabulary of emotions that we feel over and over again, but every felt sense is different.

You can however start with an emotion, and then feel the felt sense of it, as you are feeling it in your body right now.

This process of sensing takes time. So ideally there is a willingness to take that time, to wait, at the edge of not-yet-knowing what this is, patient, accepting, curious, and open.

Slowly, you sense more. This can be a bit like coming into a darkened room and sitting, and as your eyes get used to the lower light, you sense more there than you had before. You could also have come into that room and then rushed away again, not caring to sense anything there. It is the caring to, the interest, the wanting to get to know it, that brings the further knowing.

There is not a trying to change anything. There is no doing something *to* anything. In this sense, this process is very *accepting*. We accept that this felt sense is here, just as it is, right now. We are interested in *how* it is. We want to know it, just as it is.

Yet there is something more than just accepting. In this *interested curious* inner attention, there is also a confident expectation that this felt sense will change in its own way, and that it will do something that Gene Gendlin calls "making steps." What is "making steps"?

The inner world is never static. When you bring awareness to it, it unfolds, moves, becomes its next step.

An Example

A woman is Focusing, let's say, on a heavy feeling in her chest which she feels is connected with a relationship with a friend. The Focuser recently left her job, and she has just discovered that the friend is applying for the position. She has been telling herself that this is not important, but the feeling of something wrong has persisted. Now she sits down to Focus.

She brings awareness into the throat-chest-stomach area of her body and she soon discovers this heavy feeling which has been around all week. She says hello to it. She describes it freshly: "heavy... also tight... especially in the stomach and chest." Then she sits with it to get to know it better. She is interested and curious. Notice how this interested and curious is the opposite of the telling herself that this is not important which she had been doing before. She waits, with this engaged accepting attention.

She can feel that this part of her is angry. "How could she? How could she do that?" it says about her friend. Ordinarily she would be tempted to tell herself that being angry is inappropriate, but this is *Focusing*, so she just says to this place, "I hear you," and keeps waiting. Interested and curious for the "more" that is there.

In a minute she begins to sense that this part of her is also sad. "Sad" surprises her; she didn't expect sad. She asks, "Oh, what gets you sad?" In response, she senses that it is something about being invalidated. She waits, there is more. Oh, something about not being believed! When she gets that, something about not being believed, a rush of memories comes, all the times she told her friend how difficult her boss is to work for. "It's as if she didn't believe me!" is the feeling.

Now our Focuser is feeling relief in her body. This has been a *step*. The emergence of sad after the anger was also a step. The Focusing process is a series of steps of change, in which each one brings fresh insight, and a fresh body relief, "an aha" moment! Is this the end?

She could certainly stop here. But if she wanted to continue, she would go back to the "something about not being believed" feeling and again bring to it interested curiosity. It might be that there's something special for her about not being believed, something linked to her own history, which again brings relief when it is heard and understood.

Focusing brings insight and relief, but that's not all it brings. It also brings new behaviour. In the case of this woman, we can easily imagine that her way of being with her friend will now be more open, more appropriately trusting. It may also be that other areas of her life were bound up with this "not being believed" feeling, and they too will shift after this process.

This new behaviour happens naturally, easily, without having to be done by willpower or effort. And this brings us to the third special quality of Focusing.

The third key quality or aspect which sets Focusing apart from any other method of inner awareness and personal growth is *a radical philosophy of what facilitates change*.

How do we change?

How do we *not* change?

If you are like many of the people who are drawn to Focusing, you probably feel *stuck* or *blocked* in one or more areas of your life. There is *something* about you, or your circumstances, or your feelings and reactions to things that you would like to change.

That is very natural. But let us now contrast two ways of approaching this wish to change.

One way assumes that to have something change, you must make it change. You must do something to it. We can call this the Doing/Fixing way.

The other way, which we can call the Being/Allowing way, assumes that change and flow is the natural course of things, and when something seems not to change, what it needs is attention and awareness, with an attitude of allowing it to be as it is, yet open to its next steps.

Our everyday lives are deeply permeated with the Doing/Fixing assumption. When you tell a friend about a problem, how often is their response to give you advice on fixing the problem? Many of our modern therapy methods carry this assumption as well. Cognitive therapy, for example, asks you to change your self-talk. Hypnotherapy often brings in new images and beliefs to replace the old.

So the Being/Allowing philosophy, embodied in Focusing, is a radical philosophy. It *turns around* our usual expectations and ways of viewing the world. It's as if I were to say to you that this chair you are sitting on would like to become an elephant, and if you will just give it interested attention it will begin to transform. What a wild idea! Yet that is how wild it sounds, to some deeply ingrained part of ourselves, when we are told that a fear that we have might transform into something which is not at all fear, if it is given interested attention.

When people who are involved in Focusing talk about the "wisdom of the body" this is what they mean: that the felt sense "knows" what it needs to become next, as surely as a baby knows it needs warmth and comfort and food. As surely as a radish seed knows it will grow into a radish. We never have to tell the felt sense what to become; we never have to make it change.

We just need to provide the conditions which allow it to change, like a good gardener providing light and soil and water, but not telling the radish to become a cucumber."

As you can see from the extracts above, Focusing has important insights in healing emotional pain and resolving ineffective patterns of functioning.

Focusing websites are http://www.focusing.org/ and

http://www.focusingaustralia.com/index.html

While it is traditionally done in pairs, you can learn to do this for yourself, though it does takes some discipline and commitment. It is a powerful tool for self-understanding and gentle change.

The key steps are summarised below.

The "felt sense"

- Make a quiet space for you to be comfortable and relaxed in
- Tune into your torso, throat, shoulders and head, scanning gently for "felt" experiences
- Allow these to come into your awareness slowly and gently

A special quality of engaged accepting inner attention

- Ask what needs your attention right now
- Gently invite that felt sense to be and identify what it feels like – tightness, heaviness
- Allow it to be present and be curious – give it your interested attention
- Allow whatever words to come and see what resonates (feels true) for that felt sense
- Check again between the felt sense and your words to make sure it fits comfortably
- Ask 'how' and 'what' questions to gain more knowing – what makes you (felt sense) feel heavy?
- Allow that feeling to be and again be open and relaxed about what it may show/tell
- Again ask quietly and gently what is this about? Wait for a resonance or shift

A radical philosophy of what facilitates change

- Sit with the shift and thank the body for the knowing – appreciate the shift/change and relaxation

Examples

The examples below do not use the true names of people.

1. Elizabeth was experiencing anxiety around re-meeting someone she had had a relationship with that ended rather painfully, we used focusing to tune into the gut level anxiety she was feeling. A lot of sadness and a sense of failure also were felt as heaviness in the chest and thickness in the throat and sinus/nasal passages; she hadn't been aware of these other 'layers'. So once this was in her awareness, "felt" and acknowledged, these dissipated and shifted, as did much of the anxiety.

2. Joanne was a sensitive person and experienced psychological abuse throughout her childhood from her parents and older brother. There were so many instances of feeling judged and threatened that she had difficulty working with the direct experiences so we 'focused' on her 'felt' senses enabling her to tune into her body rather than trying to tell a story. The felt sense was very consistently gut level fear and feeling unsafe with the physical sensation of pressure in her chest and butterflies in her gut.

    She said that she often did 'silly' things like giggling inappropriately when in trouble with her mother and this caused more punishment. When focusing the 'butterflies' began to feel like laughter bubbling up and she realised that she knew that her mother's response to her 'wrongs' was actually quite inappropriate and 'silly'. So while she was scared there was also a part of her that 'knew' better. Awareness of this knowing empowered her and strengthened her sense of herself as other than a victim of that abuse.

Exercises

Focusing is a practical skill that you can do in 'micro' bursts and/or in full sit down sessions. (The following text may be recorded for your use.)

1. If you have ever done breathing meditation you will know the sort of gentle attention one uses in putting your attention into your breath and breathing. Being aware of the drawing of your breath and where it is in your lungs, throat and mouth/nose is a bit like 'focusing' in that it isn't trying to control or analyse it but just allow and be with the sensations.
    a) So now be aware of your breathing…… feel where your breathing is in the cycle of in - hold and out, hold then in – hold and out etc.
    b) At the end of an out breath hold the stillness for a few seconds and that is often the 'peace' point of meditation.
    c) So when you are focusing that sense of relaxation and emptiness is a state to use for reference after focusing. A finish point if you like.
    d) Practice this breathing awareness as you sit down to focus as a way of bringing your attention into the present moment and into your body.

2. Now paying attention to the physical sensations of your body without judgement is another important skill or capacity to build.
    a) Sitting quietly and uninterrupted allow yourself to 'feel' your body. Allow any sensations to just be without having to decide if there is a 'good' or 'bad' feeling there. You don't have to decide what your response 'should' be, just accept the feeling or sensation.
    b) Gentle attention is very different to our usual approach which is more about analysis and deciding something to 'fix' a problem.
    c) You may choose to 'focus' and open up a conversation with a 'felt' sense that feels like it needs your attention, or you may just practice building this skill and your awareness of your body and your 'felt' senses.
    d) Whichever you choose, remember to take a deep breath as you finish and allow the peaceful sense of finishing fill that space and the feeling of appreciation for this experience of your being.

Your reflections

This space is for you to reflect on the ideas presented, examples and exercises – what has been useful? What have you learned about yourself? What were the challenges of using this technique?

. . . .
. . . .
. . . .
. . . .
. . . .
. . . .
. . . .
. . . .
. . . .
. . . .
. . . .
. . . .
. . . .
. . . .
. . . .
. . . .
. . . .
. . . .
. . . .
. . . .
. . . .
. . . .
. . . .
. . . .
. . . .
. . . .
. . . .
. . . .
. . . .

Chapter 5

Emotional Freedom Technique

EFT is one of a range of new energy techniques used to heal emotional and physical conditions and imbalances. Research and the experience of many practitioners is showing consistent results for long-term anxiety, depression, post-trauma stress disorder, phobias, stress and insomnia with this technique.

Based on the ancient principles of acupuncture, EFT is a simple tapping procedure that clears or releases emotional and physical symptoms; the current interpretation is that it gently realigns the body's energy system, without the discomfort of needles. However, we don't really know how it works, just as the effectiveness of acupuncture itself is not well understood.

The way I understand it is that the Meridian end points used in EFT relate to organs of the body that align with strong emotions. For instance, the point under the eye relates to the stomach and fear. The collar bone point relates to the heart and feelings of loss/sadness and happiness. The underarm point is for the spleen and relates to anger. The points under the nose and below the mouth (chin point) relate to mental disorder. The eyebrow and outer corner of the eye points relate to many meridians.

Tapping is a way of sending a vibration down the energy lines and tapping on all seven points clears the meridian energy lines through the body and consequently the emotional content.

EFT is effective for an individual user, and for more persistent problems, practitioner support may be needed. It can replace years of therapy in several sessions and relieve major physical and emotional traumas and barriers. Chronic illness is also significantly reduced by regular and ongoing use of EFT.

EFT enables you to move beyond limiting feelings and behaviours.

EFT is a key piece of the puzzle for personal growth and healing. This is a tool that clears the emotional pain that drives us and defines our behaviour. It has been shown that anyone can use it from a three year old to an elder. In many cases it does not require a practitioner, and empowers us as individuals to heal ourselves of pain and trauma.

For extreme trauma and disease, it is worth working with an experienced practitioner.

Check out <u>Gary Craig's website</u> for many success stories; watch Nick Ortner's film 'Try it on Everything" (now called "The Tapping Solution") or just try it on yourself. You can also find Jessica Ortner's YouTube tapping guide.

This is a technique that has the capacity to heal individuals and communities, enabling them to live full and happy lives relieved of dysfunctional emotions and trauma. The range of issues includes everything from a bad experience at school to terrible memories of war; from sexual abuse to car accidents.

In the last decade a number of experienced practitioners have trained and worked with local health providers in disaster areas to help villagers, communities and individuals to recover from these traumas. Nick Ortner provided similar services after the Newtown shootings.

Once you have access to your feelings and experiences through your diary and/or focusing you can use the tapping process to resolve pain.

There are some things to remember.

We tend to accumulate negative experiences in our energy systems over the length of our lives; the longer we have lived the more negative "stuff" we carry around. There are often repeating patterns to our experience. Early abuse in our lives can create ways of functioning that perpetuate abusive relationships. So there can be layers of experience behind the problems we face today.

For example, dealing with a bully in the workplace can become a huge issue for someone who grew up with bullying or abuse. What might, for someone else, require a firm standing up for themselves, for the previously abused or bullied person, it becomes loaded with feelings of inadequacy and fear. Until these are relieved they cannot deal well with another's power plays.

We live in a society that believes fundamentally in the power of the human mind to understand and change. Yet we also see around us the consequences of unresolved emotional pain and trauma in day-to-day experiences from road rage to increasing drug use.

EFT is not a quick fix but it is quicker and more effective than many more traditional measures. We still have to take responsibility for our emotional and mental health. We need to develop our awareness of the patterns of thinking and feeling that drive us, often subconsciously.

But slowly and respectfully we can become aware of the pieces of our painful past and experiences, and resolve them with the tapping process.

My experience with EFT

I had worked with Journaling and Focusing for some years and felt I had achieved some progress in resolving an early childhood trauma and family neglect when I found EFT.

My experience since 2006 when I purchased Gary Craig's DVD training series has truly turned my life around in achieving peace of mind. I still use my journal and the focusing technique in conjunction with EFT, but it is EFT that has exponentially improved my results. I have noticed that cleared aspects stay cleared and it is usually another layer or issue that I am working with. I clearly had a lot of STUFF!!

This is a profound tool for self-help and healing. I cannot recommend it enough and am a passionate advocate for EFT in delivering emotional, mental and physical healing.

Practicalities

EFT involves tapping on seven meridian endpoints on the face and upper body.

Tapping these <u>in a set sequence</u> helps you keep yourself tuned in to the emotion or feelings but it is not necessary for the efficacy of the technique.

You must be tuned into a feeling, either emotional or physical, in the body and stay focused (different to the Focusing technique) on *one aspect* at a time. Using a phrase such as "….. tightness in my chest….' or 'this heavy, sadness in heart area….' helps you stay with the feelings.

We have a tendency to push our feelings down into our stomachs, so it can take some concentration and discipline to stay with a feeling or aspect of a painful experience. But doing so, will pay huge dividends in removing that pain. Practicing the Focusing technique can help you achieve this discipline.

Each experience is made up of several and sometimes many aspects. For instance, someone's experience of a car crash may be run like a movie, with some instances having more power than others. Some feeling states such as anxiety can be made up from multiple experiences with many aspects to them.

Think of the tapping as making adjustments to your energy system. How many parts make up your life, body and emotional experience? This is work of many small pieces; not a large scale wiping away of pain. Paying attention to yourself is the key to gaining the maximum results for your effort with tapping.

The next step in the process is to check your inner experience for the specific aspect and get a feel for the *intensity of it on a scale of zero to ten*, from completely gone to maximum intensity. This is so you know when the intensity comes down and to what level. You always want to leave your tapping session with no emotional content, always get it down to zero. Each aspect of a particular experience needs to be cleared completely.

Tapping through the seven points in continuous rounds while recalling an experience, is critical. Specific aspects such as the feeling of being airborne or the car hitting a tree may require specific attention and a number of rounds to clear. Persistence and willingness to stay with the experience will achieve results.

The prompt sheet below is a good resource to keep by you when you begin. Print and laminate it so you can easily find it.

EFT Basic Recipe

Tapping Points

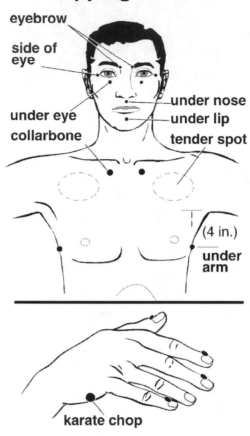

I. The Sequence. Tap each of the following points 5-7 times while tuning in to the painful feeling and saying the reminder statement. Use a short statement such as "This (insert your issue)". Example; "This fear of snakes" or "My anger at mother", "The pain in my lower back", "This anxiety about sister's visit" etc.

Here are the points to tap on:

1. **EB**= Eyebrow point, at the beginning of the eyebrow, just above and to the side of the nose.

2. **SE**= Side of the Eye, on the bone bordering the outside of the eye.

3. **UE**= Under the Eye, on the bone directly under the eye.

4. **UN**= Under Nose, in the centre of the area between the nose and top lip.

5. **Ch**= Chin, in the centre between the bottom lip and bottom of the chin.

6. **CB**= Collar bone, the junction where the collarbone, sternum and rib first meet.

7. **UA**= Under the Arm, on the side of the body approximately 4 inches below the armpit.

II. Subsequent Rounds

Once you have completed the first round of tapping, reassess your intensity level and note the change. If the problem is less severe, but still noticeable, change the reminder phrase to something like this: "*still some remaining (whatever the issue is ....)*" and continue the tapping sequence.

Keep repeating this procedure until the intensity on the issue has dropped below a 3. Check that the reminder phrase or statement is still tuning you into the feeling and adapt it so that it does.

It may change slightly to "this remaining feeling of (*whatever the issue is…*) or you may become aware that the feeling has changed. Make sure that the issue you were working on *initially* is cleared or down to zero before moving on to another aspect.

Here's a summary of everything to help bring it home….

Tuning into the issue and related feeling to identify the reminder phrase or statement.

Tap all points down to the under arm point while saying the reminder statement.

Check to see how you feel on the 1-10 scale.

Check that your reminder statement is still accurate.

Continue through to the under arm point while saying reminder statement. Check again to see how intensely you feel on the issue.

Always keep going until you're at a zero of intensity. Completely overcoming an issue will likely keep the issue from returning.

Note: If you get stuck or find you're not getting the results you want, then you may be 1) experiencing a sensitivity to a substance that's blocking your progress or 2) be dehydrated.

Try this: Tap on the karate chop point while repeating 3 times: "Even though I Don't Want to Get Over this Problem, I accept myself completely," I know, it may seem odd, but try it, it usually works, unless you have one of the other 2 conditions mentioned above.

If you still don't get any change in the feeling you may need to talk to an EFT practitioner.

Other tips:

- For tapping, use the index finger, middle finger and ring finger, at least, or all four fingers are fine.
- Tap on both sides of your body when possible.
- Do EFT while undisturbed (turn off your mobile phone)

Examples

The examples below do not use the true names of people.

1. I was on my way to a work meeting. I have never liked meetings! The firm I was working with arranged quarterly meetings for networking and reviewing practices. As I was driving and grumbling to myself about the whole exercise, I decided to tap as I was getting myself in a knot about it. After tapping through several rounds on being grumpy, anticipating frustration and feeling imposed upon, I realised that not going to meetings was really about not liking the work and kind of protesting through resistance. As I tapped through all of that, while still driving, I felt a weight lift. I had taken up the work out of a feeling that I didn't have many choices and that was just a lens through which I was seeing the world. The meeting was just fine and I wasn't sitting wishing I was elsewhere.

2. Liz had been experiencing quite debilitating panic attacks while shopping and as she was both a foster mother and mother to her own children (5 in total) she had to shop quite a lot. She said she felt quite overwhelmed with terror and often had to just leave everything in the trolley and walk out of the supermarket. Even when the children were with her the attacks persisted.
   As we worked together to distil the triggers for the panic it became clear that there were certain visual cues such as narrow or dead-end aisles that brought the fear flooding through her. So we started tapping through these triggers with varied results. The intensity would drop and then go up again when we tested by having her recall the situation. It was quite distressing for Liz so there was something more underpinning these triggers.
   I asked her to just sit with the anxiety, close her eyes and allow the feeling state to be present without trying to resist or push it away emotionally. What came up after several minutes of silence was her sobbing and the memories of her father's sexual abuse as a young girl and her sense of confinement and having no escape in confined spaces. As she cried I had her tapping through the points as I tapped on her finger points as well. It took some time as these were disturbing memories and strong kinaesthetic experiences but eventually she reported feeling empty and quite drained but lighter. She reported some months later that she had only one small re-occurrence as she was cleaning out a small dark cupboard and was able to tap the anxiety away for herself.

3. Claire had left her husband of 30 years. They had been involved in one of the major fundamentalist religions and she left because she was finding it more and more oppressive. Her children had left home and were having children of their own. Claire was dealing with her ex-husband's repeated bullying efforts to get her to return and her own bewilderment that she had stayed so long and allowed herself to be subsumed into the cult-like culture and lost her sense of self. Her children were also taking sides and this was quite distressing to her. She had found herself a good job and accommodation but was still distressed by her own depression and anxiety even after having escaped the marriage and church environments.

We worked on these over some months and she started to feel better but each interaction with a family member seemed to re-trigger her despair and sense of powerlessness. In one session she recalled suddenly a particular event from her youth that was extremely intense. We tapped through her description of returning home after taking up a job in a major city some distance from her rural family home, where her father came to pick her up from the train. As they were driving along he casually tried to sexually assault her saying she was now a grown up woman. She had forgotten this incident but realised it had a powerful impact on her life and partner choices. Her despair and sense of being exploited arose from this experience and enabled others to trigger that same behaviour pattern.

I had her focus on the *felt sense* of gut-wrenching fear and anguish and tap through the story until it dissipated. She still had some very difficult family dynamics to get through but was able to handle them without feeling guilty or frightened. People were not able to push that button any longer and she reported that they seemed less confident that they could bully her.

4. I had a traumatic event as a young child when I spent 2 weeks in hospital being stuck with needles and held down by adults. While my parents came every day my senses of abandonment and loss were profound and impacted on my development as a child and young adult.

    Much of my personal work has been in clearing the many painful aspects of this experience from terror of being held tightly to having difficulty trusting anyone. Much of this work has been from the non-verbal kinaesthetic experiences in childhood and required discipline and persistence to work through. This latter has been some of the most difficult as I had no words to articulate the physical experiences and had to just trust that what I felt was enough to enable the tapping to work and it did.

    As an example I woke up one night in terror as my bed coverings had somehow tightened around me and I felt I couldn't breathe or escape. So I sat up and allowing myself to feel the panic and fear, tapped and tapped. It was quite hard to hold myself to the fear as it felt overwhelming. After about 45 minutes of working through the layers of claustrophobia, the physical sensation of being unable to move and being held and almost crushed under something, the feeling of extreme panic subsided. I was then able to work through expanding my breathing and movements. I haven't had this sensation since and find myself able to relax and trust that I can stand up for myself. I feel empowered to act for myself.

Exercises

There are two exercises used for giving new 'tappers' a stress-free experience with the technique.

1. Most of us have **constricted breathing,** where we only draw air into the upper part of our lungs. This is due to life stress and a lack of awareness.
   a) So take as deep a breath as you can and estimate on a scale of zero to ten (ten being fully filling your lungs) how much you have filled your lungs;
   b) Putting your attention into your lungs and feeling the constriction there, tap through several rounds, then take another breath as deeply as you can and estimate as before how fully you have filled your lung capacity.
   c) It is usual for the filled capacity to increase by several points; continue tapping until you have filled your lungs to capacity several times.

2. We also hold stress and tension in our upper backs, shoulders, necks and back of our heads.
   a) So putting your attention into this area, estimate on a scale of zero to ten, ten being maximum tension or tightness in the back, neck and head.
   b) Again putting your attention into this area, feel the tension or tightness there, tap through several rounds, then take breath and estimate as before how much tension you feel.
   c) It is usual for the tension to reduce by several points so continue tapping until you have no tension in this area.

3. Think about someone in your life that frustrates or annoys you. It may be someone you live or work with or perhaps someone that your see only occasionally but who still manages to quickly annoy you.
   a) As you think of them and perhaps your last interaction with them, scan your body for sensations. Has your gut knotted or your throat tightened?
   b) Just spend a few seconds getting a sense of your responses and then estimate how intensely you are reacting on a scale of zero to ten. Note this point. Is there a word or phrase that expresses this experience? Note these as well.
   c) Take a deep breath and allow yourself to connect to and tune into this feeling state while repeating the words or phrase internally. Make sure that the words enable you to keep tuning into the feeling state.
   d) Tap through the points several times while staying tuned into the feeling state. Take a deep breath and check your intensity and note this.
   e) Keep tapping until the intensity for this issue has gone.
   f) Take a deep breath and allow yourself to feel the absence of tension or physical symptoms.

Your reflections

This space is for you to reflect on the ideas presented, examples and exercises – what has been useful? What have you learned about yourself? You may transfer these to your journal to further tease out the ideas and reflections.

. . . .
. . . .
. . . .
. . . .
. . . .
. . . .
. . . .
. . . .
. . . .
. . . .
. . . .
. . . .
. . . .
. . . .
. . . .
. . . .
. . . .
. . . .
. . . .
. . . .
. . . .
. . . .
. . . .
. . . .
. . . .
. . . .
. . . .
. . . .
. . . .
. . . .
. . . .

Chapter 6

INTEGRATION

I hope by now you have learned and practised each of the three techniques and have started to use all three together in some form.

In this chapter I will provide some micro-processes for integrating the three techniques as well as identifying critical issues for yourself.

You have choices about how you approach your inner work. You can;

1. Work with your current experience of issues and allow the layers to arise in an organic way. So that you are responding to your direct and current experiences by reflecting and releasing <u>as</u> you uncover or reveal uncomfortable emotions
    or

2. Map out your issues using one of the following processes for analysing and identifying issues and work through these progressively
    or

3. Use a combination of both

I recommend that you start out with option number 1 if there are issues that you are aware of now. If you are feeling depressed or anxious, work with these feelings directly. The life line process may be useful in this case.

If your experience is less intense or pressing then do one of the exercises such as life map, mind mapping or life line to begin to identify potential issues for your inner work.

If you are feeling okay but are not satisfied with a particular aspect of your life, such as work success then unpacking your experience and the factors influencing your current state using the mind mapping process could be most useful.

Remember that you are unique and there is no right way for every person in this process of inner work. If there are problems in your outer life than these are often reflections of some inner limitation or block.

Your process of inner work will develop over time and you will find what works for you.

REFLECTION FRAMEWORK

This framework is designed to help you understand how these techniques work together to progress you through your personal development and healing. The knowledge resources and conceptual models set out in the last chapter will help you better understand your experiences.

This framework is based on a *process* of learning and reflection cycles using the techniques moving through *journaling, shifting to focusing and then on to tapping.*

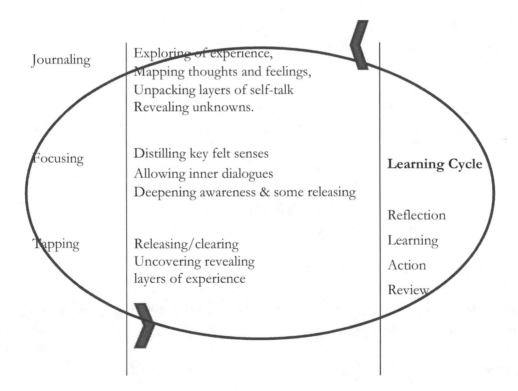

Integrated Healing Process

Using these techniques in a reflective cycle enables you to *complete and resolve* an issue. Working through the techniques on an issue and back to journaling *is* a learning cycle. The result is that you quite naturally shift into the *action* stage of the learning cycle because the learning is completed.

By establishing this integrated learning sequence, as a personal practice, we can move through a variety of relevant issues, concerns and barriers knowing that we are resolving matters as deeply as we are able at this time. *Other issues may arise later on, but we can only work on the layers of experience and problems we are aware of, at this time.*

It is very important to be compassionate and caring of ourselves through this process.

We often want quick results and can become impatient to get clear and over these blocks. However, it may have taken your whole life to develop these problems, and working too quickly can reduce your effectiveness and motivation. You need to remain disciplined in your inner work. Don't allow the cultural self-talk about 'getting over it" to undermine your progress and process. Take care of yourself on your journey.

Integration Exercises

The exercises for this chapter are more comprehensive than in the previous chapters. We are integrating these techniques;

- As a personal development process
- With a range of micro-processes involving analysis and mapping of your life
- And learning conceptual maps & personal development knowledge

Are you ready?

Remember take it slow, be kind to yourself (don't judge yourself harshly) and remember there are no right answers; this is your life journey.

You will need to access the maps and models chapter, your journal and this chapter.

Firstly read through the summary of processes and identify one that resonates for you and/ or seems most useful at this point.

Core Processes

Process	Use to:
Life sectors map	Self-assess what area of your life needs priority inner work
Life Line Review	Overview the highs & lows in your journey, the links & potential issues
Mind Mapping	Extract/distil the details & links for your situation
Specific Event Story	Work on specific events

1. **Life Sectors map**. The different life sectors are shown below and you are reviewing each sector of your life for your level of satisfaction and deciding where you need to start your inner work.

   The sectors are as follows:

Relationships	0—-1---2—-3—-4----5—-6—-7--8-—9---10
Family/friends	0—-1---2—-3—-4----5—-6—-7--8-—9---10
Work/career	0—-1---2—-3—-4----5—-6—-7--8-—9---10
Education	0—-1---2—-3—-4----5—-6—-7--8-—9---10
Recreation/fun	0—-1---2—-3—-4----5—-6—-7--8-—9---10
Spirituality/growth	0—-1---2—-3—-4----5—-6—-7--8-—9---10
Health/wellbeing	0—-1---2—-3—-4----5—-6—-7--8-—9---10
Financial security	0—-1---2—-3—-4----5—-6—-7--8-—9---10
Physical environment	0—-1---2—-3—-4----5—-6—-7--8-—9---10

Ask yourself – what is your level of satisfaction on each of these sectors on a scale of 0 to 10 with ten being absolute satisfaction? Think and feel your sense of each sector; what do they mean to you? Do they feel good or uncomfortable?

Draw in your journal a sectored circle with the above headings and mark your positions for each of these sectors.

You may find that many are linked and have similar underlying issues and formative experiences.

Which one is the most pressing need for action and resolution?

In your **journal** begin to unpack its importance in your life, what beliefs you may have inherited from your family and what action you have taken. Has this worked in achieving your desired outcomes? What is this about and what stops you from moving forward easily in resolving this concern?

Check into your body for a felt sense; where is it in your body? Spend some time **focusing** and having an inner dialogue with this felt sense. Record this experience in your journal and what shifts you may have experienced.

When these feel unresolved or persistent start **tapping** for several rounds and tune into where the felt sense may be stuck in your body. Are there some words that resonate with that feeling state?

You may find Louise Hay's book "You Can Heal Your Life" and Annette Noontill's useful for identifying the meaning of certain disease or chronic problems.

Additional maps in chapter 7 that could be useful are;

- Force field analysis
- Maslow's hierarchy of need

You may find that as you work through these questions and processes that you get diverted by what seems like a particularly pressing matter; trust your own instincts for what is really important.

Sometimes we need to go through several loops of exploration that may not *seem* useful but do finally take you to something critical.

Sometimes we simply cannot directly confront an issue and must *sneak* up on it. There may be too many layers of family injunctions about dealing with messy family business or it may be just too painful. Allow yourself to keep to an organic pace rather than like a train busting through. Be determined and disciplined but not hard or harsh on yourself.

As you work through the life map circle using the *journal to focusing to tapping* processes there may be some things that you flag for yourself to come back to when you have time and energy. It isn't a race. Life is full of tantalising side roads.

Some issues you may identify for later work are;

- Family dynamics and patterns of behaviour that you have inherited and find cause you difficulties in your own home, family or working life
- Life events that have been formative for you and have been mostly useful but sometimes not

Please take your time in doing this exercise. Appreciate the positives in your life as well as working on what needs to be done.

2. **Life Line Review**

Start a line in your journal at your birth and extend it to your current age across the page. Identify what the highs and lows have been on the line. For example, parental break up, leaving home or school, major business successes, birth of your own children, health problems, job changes or achievements; whatever is relevant to your life.

Example   Now

| 0 | 5 | 10 | 15 | 20 | 30 | 40 | 50 | |

Parents divorced

lived with grandparents

Left school to work in family business

Married

What have been the impacts?

How did you feel at the time, what did you think?

What are your responses now? Have you buried those feelings and thoughts?

Unpack some of the key or critical ones in your journal. What still needs work?

Are there particular 'voices' from your family or life experiences that still direct you or wheedle you into certain behaviour or actions?

In your journal identify these and allow them to speak freely. Ask them what do they need and how do they think what they are telling you will be helpful?

Aunt Millie may have a morbid fear of going out at night after some terrible incident in her childhood and wants to protect you. Even though you are grown up and a martial arts expert!! Allow her to speak and explain her experience and concerns; otherwise she is likely to just nag you at a negative self-talk level.

Dialoguing with these people from your past can unpack some interesting "writing on your walls". Gary Craig who developed EFT uses this term to highlight the inner dialogues and instructions that are part of all of us.

At this point you could do some *focusing* to open up to your felt senses and see if there is something your body's wisdom can bring you. It might be enough to allow it to speak its piece and accept that as part of your make-up.

If it seems that this voice or being is more powerful than that and perhaps negative in impact you can start tapping on the sense of fear or perhaps some more specific words that it has resonated with.

Make further notes in your journal about this inner exchange, the felt sense and tapping through experiences.

You may find that in resolving this fear or anxiety, that **other related issues** from before and after that particular incident arise for you to also work through. So journal, trust your felt senses and tap!

This exercise as with the Life Map one can be foundation processes to come back to. Something that happens tomorrow or a year from now may recall an event in your teens and this is a signal to revisit your life line exercise to unpack further that experience. Trust your instincts to follow through and be gentle with yourself.

And if you get or feel stuck either *focus* on the stuck feeling or *tap*.

3. Specific Event Story telling

For some there will be *one significant event* that has impacted on your life or perhaps a series of them of a similar nature.

In your journal write your version of the event and how it impacted on you at the time. Tell it as a story, identifying each person involved, what happened and particular points of action that impacted on you.

You may have told this story many times and sometimes it's hard to feel what you felt then… so *focus* on your *body senses* as you write. Where is there tension and fear? Be open to those feelings and senses even as they may cause you discomfort or distress. What messages do your *felt* senses have for you?

Write down the sequence of events, allowing your body senses to be in your awareness and tap on each aspect that has any intense feeling or discomfort associated with it.

Remember to estimate the intensity on the 0 to 10 scale so you can track that those intense feelings are reducing or changing as you move through the story.

You can tap on the whole event and each point in the story of your experience to clear up each aspect. You then need to **test the effectiveness by thinking about the event** to see if there is any *discomfort or distress* remaining. Another aspect may come into your awareness or another felt sense in your body may need further focusing and tapping.

Stay with it even as you again experience the distress. It may feel overwhelming but it is just feelings; there is no *real* physical threat to you as there was when you first experienced this event.

Persistence and discipline are necessary to clear painful abuse and trauma.

This is the part most people find difficult. They have probably done many things to avoid these feelings over the years and this behaviour has become a set pattern.

You may find that some of your avoidance strategies cause other problems such as addictions. If you find it too difficult by yourself find a counsellor you can work with.

4. Mind mapping exercise

Take a large sheet of paper or use a large whiteboard. In the centre of the space write your name. What is the focus of your life, work or concerns right now? What are the symptoms?

A **mind map** is a diagram used to visually organise information. It is often created around a single concept, drawn as an image in the centre of a blank landscape page, to which associated representations of ideas such as images, words and parts of words are added.

Major ideas are connected directly to the central concept, and other ideas branch out from those.

My mind mapping for my current situation allowed me to see the journey of change I had been on and appreciate the shifts in direction and challenges. It helped process some inner work about communications with family, and how I wanted to contribute to my new community.

Your reflection

This space is for you to reflect on the ideas and exercises; what has been useful? What have you learned about yourself? You may transfer these to your journal to further tease out the ideas and reflections.

. . . .
. . . .
. . . .
. . . .
. . . .
. . . .
. . . .
. . . .
. . . .
. . . .
. . . .
. . . .
. . . .
. . . .
. . . .
. . . .
. . . .
. . . .
. . . .
. . . .
. . . .
. . . .
. . . .
. . . .
. . . .
. . . .
. . . .
. . . .
. . . .
. . . .
. . . .
. . . .

Chapter 7

MAPS AND MODELS

This section provides ideas and concepts that will help you understand yourself and your experience better. They are ways of seeing yourself, your situation and how others may behave, but they are not the whole truth. Your experience and judgement are necessary to make sense of it and decide what is relevant to you.

Summary

Maps & Models	Use to:
Force field Analysis	Identify the forces holding you stuck in your current situation & what needs what kind of action
Maslow's Hierarchy of Needs	Identify your priority needs & gaps
Psychological framework Subconscious/awareness	Psychological aspects to human inner work and outer behaviour
Inventory of concerns & Focus of control	Identify all of your current concerns & then determine what you are actually responsible for
Learning Cycle & styles **Competency Model**	Identify your style & where you may be missing learning opportunities Learning stages
Personality Type Indicators	Identify your personality preferences
Role Theory	What roles do you play & how effective are they?
Transactional Analysis	Identify relationship positions
Neurolinguistic Programming	Identify how effective your communication style is with others

Force field analysis

This model is often used in managing organisational change but is also useful for understanding your own personal dynamics in changing your behaviour and thinking and feeling processes.

If you are working with a pattern of behaviour that isn't effective for you but is proving hard to change, you could find there are actually some 'pay-offs' for you in maintaining the status quo. Some patterns of thinking and feeling can hold us stuck so mapping out what driving and restraining forces may be operating is useful.

The model asks you to look at how you could increase the driving forces and reduce the restraining forces.

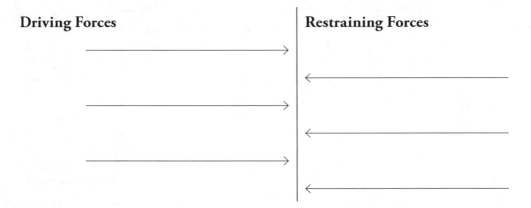

So in a personal setting where you want to change how you respond to someone being directive and your feelings of frustration you might map out the following analysis for yourself.

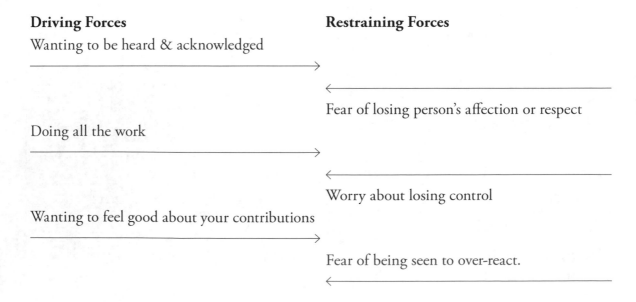

Looking at each of these issues to see how you could improve them is a first step to changing this dynamic. It also helps you identify where your weaknesses and strengths are in the situation.

Psychological framework

The human being is surely one of the most psychologically complex beings on this planet. Though other species may have similar intelligence they don't seem to suffer the complex range of inner impulses and drivers for thinking, feeling and behaviour that we do.

Carl G Jung developed the notion of the <u>Collective Unconscious</u> as a way of describing the powerful collective/common themes that all cultures develop through their art, stories and drama such as archetypes; 'Earth Mother' or 'Trickster' may be a common ones. It is like a hard-wired cultural framework that we hold in common and resonates to shared stories or art.

That many different cultures value similar cultural relics or expressions is indicative of this commonality. It is also a learning strategy that we have by preference; tell me a story, show me a picture, play a piece of music or sing a song.

We understand at a deep level the meaning of culture and we resonate to these expressions.

We also have a *"personal unconscious"* that has developed through our life experiences and while we may be consciously aware of some events and experiences, we often are not aware of how these have programmed us to behave and respond to either our external experiences or our inner dynamics. We often disassociate ourselves from painful experiences and 'forget' them so we don't have to deal with the pain or distress of them. But they live in us through reactions that we don't seem to have any control over; often taking the form of destructive impulses, addictions and chronic disease and pain. We are often quite unaware of how we behave and why. The Human Shadow is another term for this personal unconscious.

Another level of the unconscious is the specific programs and learned behaviour, beliefs and attitudes from our family and key people through our life about who we are. It is like a life script and relates to birth order, multi-generational patterning as well as the modelling related to relationships, work, learning and self-worth.

From About.com.psychology the following are definitions of key aspects of human psychology from Carl Jung's work.

Projection is a defence mechanism that involves taking our own unacceptable qualities or feelings and ascribing them to other people. For example, if you have a strong dislike for someone, you might instead believe that he or she does not like you. Projection works by allowing the expression of the desire or impulse, but in a way that the ego cannot recognize, therefore reducing anxiety. Or perhaps you dislike someone and unconsciously regard them as having a particular attribute you dislike in yourself.

The Self

The self is an archetype that represents the unification of the unconsciousness and consciousness of an individual. The creation of the self occurs through a process known as individuation, in which the various aspects of personality are integrated.

The Shadow

The shadow is an archetype that consists of the sex and life instincts. The shadow exists as part of the unconscious mind and is composed of repressed ideas, weaknesses, desires, instincts and shortcomings. This archetype is often described as the darker side of the psyche, representing wildness, chaos and the unknown. These latent dispositions are present in all of us, Jung believed, although people sometimes deny this element of their own psyche and instead project it onto others.

Jung suggested that the shadow can appear in dreams or visions and may take a variety of forms. It might appear as a snake, a monster, a demon, a dragon or some other dark, wild or exotic figure.

The Anima or Animus

The anima is a feminine image in the male psyche and the animus is a male image in the female psyche. The anima/animus represents the "true self" rather than the image we present to others and serves as the primary source of communication with the collective unconscious.

The combination of the anima and animus is known as the syzygy, or the divine couple. The syzygy represents completion, unification and wholeness.

The Persona

The persona is how we present ourselves to the world. The word "persona" is derived from a Latin word that literally means "mask." It is not a literal mask, however. The persona represents all of the different social masks that we wear among different groups and situations. It acts to shield the ego from negative images. According to Jung, the persona may appear in dreams and take a number of different forms.

Maslow's hierarchy of need

This concept relates to how and why people are motivated to act. Abraham Maslow theorised that people must have satisfied their lower level survival needs before they can act to satisfy higher order needs. This has been found to be not entirely true but the concept does give a good map of the factors that influence our decisions and actions.

Self-fulfilment; being able to enact one's full capacity as a human being, spiritual growth and creative contributions to life

Status; having a place in family, work and community, respect and standing

Social; belonging to a family or community, engaging with others on common activities and interests

Security; reliable resources for staying alive – not having to worry about one's next meal or where one might sleep

Physiological/survival needs; food, shelter & safety from threats

Inventory of concerns exercise

Most of us have many things in our lives to do or be or manage or influence. Sometimes these can feel quite overwhelming and immobilising as we try to decide what to do next.

Make a list of concerns and include the whole shebang! From your dad's birthday celebration to your daughter's graduation to training a new person at work. Some are positive but they still take effort and energy. Writing them all down can stop all that stuff running constantly through your mind.

Now identify which ones are under your control and which ones you can influence and which you have no control or influence over.

Give yourself permission where there is a concern you have no control or influence over, to just let it go. You don't need to carry stress or tension in your body or life for things you have no control over; unless there is a major threat to your life or family and it truly requires fight or flight action.

Learning cycle

This model is a useful way of understanding how people develop skills and explains the different types of activity to be effective learners. We can review and use this model when things don't quite work out as we planned.

| Reflection | > | theory | > | planning | > |
| action | > | reflection | > | theory |

Reflection may involve seeking feedback from others and reviewing your assumptions (theories) about what would work and why. You may then speculate on another theory or even do some research before planning your next action.

In our personal lives we often operate on 'automatic' pilot or old programming from family experiences. Reflection may require reviewing what worked or not in those environments.

Learning styles

Individuals have preferences for different stages of the learning cycle and this can impact on their capacity to learn and develop skills and awareness beyond their current level. Being aware of your approach to the learning process will be important to further developing additional skills of learning in your life.

People with preferences for;

Action will enjoy new experiences, excitement and drama and being thrown in the deep end. Those with low preference for action may plan and theorise and review events but their capacity for spontaneous, unplanned activity is lower.

Reflection will enjoy standing back, listening and observing, thinking before acting, reviewing and analysing events but those with low preference for reflection tend not to observe and evaluate events and often fail to build on experience and repeat failures.

Theory will enjoy exploring ideas and concepts, relating specific events to theories while those with low preferences for theory will have difficulty in reaching conclusions and gaining value from principles thus fail to understand similarities and differences in situations.

Planning will enjoy learning about techniques with practical use, learning directly from role models, putting skills into practice while those with a lesser preference for planning will arrive at events and interaction unprepared having not thought ahead about requirements.

Competency Model

While learning a new skill, it is important to understand that there are stages in the development process. The first stage is a state of *unconscious incompetence* where we are unaware of the skill area and we don't know what we don't know.

The second stage is *conscious incompetence* where we become aware of what we don't know.

The third stage is *conscious competence* where we have learned a new skill set and we can explain what the key principles and practices and can demonstrate their application with congruence.

The fourth stage is *unconscious competence* where the acquisition and application of those skills has become internalised and second nature so that we operate unconsciously.

Personality Type Indicators

With all the diversity of human personality and preferences, it is useful to understand some of the dimensions of difference and similarities. Sometimes when we have conflicts with other people it isn't because they are bad or wrong but that they have different strengths from us.

One useful model is the Myer-Briggs Personality Type Indicator. There are questionnaires for this, however just understanding the different dimensions is helpful to working with others.

This model is based on Carl Jung's work and was developed over several decades by a mother and daughter team.

There are four dimensions:

Introversion – Extroversion;

Sensate – Intuition;

Feeling (values) – Thinking (analysis);

Judging – Perception.

Below explanation is extracted from Wikipedia.

Note that the terms used for each dimension have specific technical meanings relating to the MBTI which differ from their everyday usage. For example, people who prefer judgment over perception are not necessarily more *judgmental* or less *perceptive*. Nor does the MBTI instrument measure aptitude; it simply indicates for one preference over another. Someone reporting a high score for extraversion over introversion cannot be correctly described as *more* extraverted: they simply have a clear *preference*.

Point scores on each of the dimensions can vary considerably from person to person, even among those with the same type. However, Isabel Myers considered the *direction* of the preference (for example, E vs. I) to be more important than the *degree* of the preference (for example, very clear vs. slight). The expression of a person's psychological type is more than the sum of the four individual preferences. The preferences interact through *type dynamics* and *type development*.

Attitudes: extraversion/introversion (E/I)

Myers-Briggs literature uses the terms *extraversion* and *introversion* as Jung first used them. Extraversion means "outward-turning" and introversion means "inward-turning". These specific definitions vary somewhat from the popular usage of the words. Note that *extraversion* is the spelling used in MBTI publications.

The preferences for extraversion and introversion are often called "attitudes". Briggs and Myers recognized that each of the cognitive functions can operate in the external world of behaviour, action, people, and things ("extraverted attitude") or the internal world of ideas and reflection ("introverted attitude"). The MBTI assessment sorts for an overall preference for one or the other.

People who prefer extraversion draw energy from action: they tend to act, then reflect, then act further. If they are inactive, their motivation tends to decline. To rebuild their energy, extraverts need breaks from time spent in reflection. Conversely, those who prefer introversion "expend" energy through action: they prefer to reflect, then act, then reflect again. To rebuild their energy, introverts need quiet time alone, away from activity.

The extravert's flow is directed outward toward people and objects, and the introvert's is directed inward toward concepts and ideas. Contrasting characteristics between extraverts and introverts include the following:

- Extraverts are "action" oriented, while introverts are "thought" oriented.
- Extraverts seek "breadth" of knowledge and influence, while introverts seek "depth" of knowledge and influence.
- Extraverts often prefer more "frequent" interaction, while introverts prefer more "substantial" interaction.
- Extraverts recharge and get their energy from spending time with people, while introverts recharge and get their energy from spending time alone; they consume their energy through the opposite process

Functions: sensing/intuition (S/N) and thinking/feeling (T/F)

Jung identified two pairs of psychological functions:

- The two perceiving functions, sensing and intuition
- The two judging functions, thinking and feeling

According to Jung's typology model, each person uses one of these four functions more dominantly and proficiently than the other three; however, all four functions are used at different times depending on the circumstances.

Sensing and *intuition* are the information-gathering (perceiving) functions. They describe how new information is understood and interpreted. Individuals who prefer *sensing* are more likely to trust information that is in the present, tangible, and concrete: that is, information that can be understood by the five senses. They tend to distrust hunches, which seem to come "out of nowhere". They prefer to look for details and facts. For them, the meaning is in the data. On the other hand, those who prefer *intuition* tend to trust information that is more abstract or theoretical, that can be associated with other information (either remembered or discovered by seeking a wider context or pattern). They may be more interested in future possibilities. For them, the meaning is in the underlying theory and principles which are manifested in the data.

Thinking and *feeling* are the decision-making (judging) functions. The thinking and feeling functions are both used to make rational decisions, based on the data received from their information-gathering functions (sensing or intuition). Those who prefer *thinking* tend to decide things from a more detached standpoint, measuring the decision by what seems reasonable, logical, causal, consistent, and matching a given set of rules. Those who prefer *feeling* tend to come to decisions by associating or empathizing with the situation, looking at it 'from the inside' and weighing the situation to achieve, on balance, the greatest harmony, consensus and fit, considering the needs of the people involved. Thinkers usually have trouble interacting with people who are inconsistent or illogical, and tend to give very direct feedback to others. They are concerned with the truth and view it as more important.

As noted already, people who prefer thinking do not necessarily, in the everyday sense, "think better" than their feeling counterparts; the opposite preference is considered an equally rational way of coming to decisions (and, in any case, the MBTI assessment is a measure of preference, not ability). Similarly, those who prefer feeling do not necessarily have "better" emotional reactions than their thinking counterparts.

According to Jung, people use all four cognitive functions. However, one function is generally used in a more conscious and confident way. This dominant function is supported by the secondary (auxiliary) function, and to a lesser degree the tertiary function. The fourth and least conscious function is always the opposite of the dominant function. Myers called this inferior function the *shadow*.

The four functions operate in conjunction with the attitudes (extraversion and introversion). Each function is used in either an extraverted or introverted way. A person whose dominant function is extraverted intuition, for example, uses intuition very differently from someone whose dominant function is introverted intuition.

Lifestyle: judging/perception (J/P)

Myers and Briggs added another dimension to Jung's typological model by identifying that people also have a preference for using either the *judging* function (thinking or feeling) or their *perceiving* function (sensing or intuition) when relating to the outside world (extraversion).

Myers and Briggs held that types with a preference for *judging* show the world their preferred judging function (thinking or feeling). So TJ types tend to appear to the world as logical, and FJ types as empathetic. According to Myers, judging types like to "have matters settled".

Those types who prefer *perception* show the world their preferred perceiving function (sensing or intuition). So SP types tend to appear to the world as concrete and NP types as abstract. According to Myers, perceptive types prefer to "keep decisions open".

For extraverts, the J or P indicates their *dominant* function; for introverts, the J or P indicates their *auxiliary* function. Introverts tend to show their dominant function outwardly only in matters "important to their inner worlds". For example:

Because the ENTJ type is extraverted, the J indicates that the *dominant* function is the preferred judging function (extraverted thinking). The ENTJ type introverts the auxiliary perceiving function (introverted intuition). The tertiary function is sensing and the inferior function is introverted feeling.

Because the INTJ type is introverted, however, the J instead indicates that the *auxiliary* function is the preferred judging function (extraverted thinking). The INTJ type introverts the dominant perceiving function (introverted intuition). The tertiary function is feeling and the inferior function is extraverted sensing.

Transactional Analysis

Eric Berne MD created the psychological theory of Transactional Analysis in the 1950s. Please check his website for comprehensive explanation of his ideas. http://www.ericberne.com/transactional-analysis/

At a simple level he identifies three 'ego states' that we have as humans; Parent, child and adult. See below for extract from his webpage.

The interesting perspective on this theory is that we can experience dysfunctional, conflicting and frustrating interactions with others because we are operating from different ego states. We may also experience complementary interactions that are still not useful such as parent to child. There may be people in your life that you always interact with in a particular way – like a pattern laid down in your programming. It may be a situation in which you end up feeling powerless – child like when you really need to be an adult and make better decisions for yourself.

Parent

The parent represents a massive collection of recordings in the brain of *external* events experienced or perceived in approximately the first five years of life. Since the majority of the external events experienced by a child are actions of the parent, the ego state was appropriately called Parent. Note that events perceived by the child from individuals that are NOT parents (but who are often in parent-like roles) are also recorded in the Parent. When Transactional Analysts refer to the Parent ego state (as opposed to a biological or stepparent), it is capitalized. The same goes for the other two states (Adult and Child).

Examples of recordings in the Parent include:

- "Never talk to strangers"
- "Always chew with your mouth closed"
- "Look both ways before you cross the street"

It is worth noting that, while recording these events, the young child has no way to filter the data; the events are recorded without question and without analysis. One can consider that these events are imposed on the child.

There are other data experienced by the child that are not recorded in the Parent. This is recorded in the Adult, which will be described shortly.

Child

In contrast to the Parent, the Child represents the recordings in the brain of *internal* events associated with external events the child perceives. Stated another way, stored in the Child are the *emotions* or *feelings* which accompanied external events. Like the Parent, recordings in the Child occur from childbirth all the way up to the age of approximately 5 years old.

Examples of recordings in the Child include:

- "When I saw the monster's face, I felt really scared"
- "The clown at the birthday party was really funny!

Adult

The Adult is the last ego state. Close to one year of age, a child begins to exhibit gross motor activity. The child learns that he or she can control a cup from which to drink, that he or she can grab a toy. In social settings, the child can play peek-a-boo.

This is the beginning of the Adult in the small child. Adult data grows out of the child's ability to see what is different than what he or she observed (Parent) or felt (Child). In other words, the Adult allows the young person to evaluate and validate Child and Parental data. Berne describes the Adult as being "principally concerned with transforming stimuli into pieces of information, and processing and filing that information on the basis of previous experience"[6] Stated another way, Harris describes the Adult as "a data-processing computer, which grinds out decisions after computing the information from three sources: the Parent, the Child, and the data which the adult has gathered and is gathering"[7]

One of the key functions of the Adult is to validate data in the parent. An example is:

"Wow. It really is true that pot handles should always be turned into the stove" said Sally as she saw her brother burn himself when he grabbed a pot handle sticking out from the stove.

In this example, Sally's Adult reached the conclusion that data in her Parent was valid. Her Parent had been taught "always turn pot handles into the stove, otherwise you could get burned." And with her analysis of her brother's experience, her Adult concluded that this was indeed correct.

Role Theory and Training defines a role as the functioning form a person's behaviour takes in response to a person or object and are about how we interact with each other. Roles imply a position, belief or attitude taken. Roles are established through;

- our own expectations and what we think we 'should' do,
- how we usually do things,
- expectations of significant others
- the behaviour and style of significant others – how they model the role

Regardless of the type of job or role, every role has four functional roles within it;

Emotional Stimulation	Caring	Meaning Attribution	Executive Function
Challenging Confronting Releasing/expressing strong emotion Intrusive modelling Catalysing interaction	Accepting Understanding Supporting Modelling warmth Developing intimate relationships	Reflecting Interpreting Explaining Labelling Linking	Gate-keeping Setting standards Giving directions Blocking Directing traffic

Roles can be;

Adequate – effective or useful and congruent
Conflicted – e.g. caring conniver, limp leader (not usually linked)

Underdeveloped – not fully used role
Overdeveloped – used too much and inappropriate
Absent – completely unavailable

It is useful to name roles as it helps us clarify what is working and what is not. Naming roles involves defining a descriptor and noun. Some options are below.

Descriptor	Noun
Critical	Bystander
Technical	Evaluator
Expert	Judger
Caring	Conniver
Confused	Dictator
Limp	Leader
Challenging	Colleague
Benevolent	Director
Concerned	Decider
Distant	Reactor
Abrupt	Carer
Interested	Observer

Role theory is useful when looking at how ineffective aspects of ourselves are expressed in our relationships and roles. For example if you are a fearful person due to early life experiences the way you behaviour in a leadership role will be negatively affected and people may experience you as less powerful in that role. You may on the other hand, be regarded as a supportive person in a team environment, due to this 'role'.

Understanding your roles can enable you to identify gaps and learning opportunities.

Neurolinguistic Programming

NLP was developed by two Americans **Richard Bandler and John Grinder**, who established with their research that the communication of highly regarded therapists involved some never previously understood brain and behaviour 'technology'. What is most useful to understand is that we take in information, process it and respond to it, from three to four different sensory modes. These differences can cause significant conflict in work teams and families as well as relationships.

These modes are visual, auditory, kinaesthetic and sometimes gustatory or olfactory. The most common are the first three, and we use different modes for taking in information, processing and responding or expressing it.

In identifying our own or another's modes, we can "influence" them, when we use *their* preferred modes in our communication.

For instance if you prefer to take in information visually and process it via an auditory function; that is talk yourself through it, and then show others by doing, you have a v-a-k process. If you use this for everyone you interact with, you will find that not everyone "gets it", because they will have a different process.

There is lots of information on the internet but some of it lacks depth. The creators of this systemic approach to communication have written many books and these are readily available in good book stores. This website is probably one of the more informative http://www.nlp.com.au/

This is a complex system of thinking about human behaviour, thinking and communication and well worth developing some awareness of.

Reading List

Louise Hay, **You Can Heal Your Life**, Hay House publishers

Annette Noontil, **The Body is the Barometer of the Soul - So be your own Doctor II**, self-published, McPherson's Printing Group

David R. Hawkins, **Power vs. Force – The Hidden Determinants of Human Behavior,** Hay House Revised edition 2002

Carolyn Myss Ph.D., **Anatomy of the Spirit – The Seven Stages of Power and Healing**, Bantam Books, 1996

Robert A. Johnson, **Inner Work – Using Dreams & Active Imagination for Personal Growth**, Harper San Francisco 1989

Robert Bly, **A Little Book on The Human Shadow**, Element Books, 1988

Anthony De Mello S.J., Edited by J. Francis Stroud, S.J., **Awareness – A de Mello Spirituality Conference in His Own Words**, Fount, Harper Collins Publishers 1990

References

Isabel Briggs Myers with Peter B. Myers, **Gifts Differing (MBTI)**, Consulting Psychologists Press, Inc., Palo Alto, CA 1980

Ann Weiser Cornell Ph.D., **The Power of Focusing – A Practical Guide to Emotional Self-Healing**, New Harbinger Publications, 1996

Ann Weiser Cornell Ph.D., **Introduction to Focusing,** Focusing Resources, 2625 Alcatraz Avenue, #202, Berkeley CA 94705-2702.

George Boak and David Thompson, **Mental Models for Managers – Frameworks for Practical Thinking**, Random House Publishers, 1998

Kay Leigh Hagan, **Internal Affairs – A Journalkeeping Workbook for Self-Intimacy**, Harper & Row Publishers, San Francisco 1990

Tristine Rainer, **The New Diary: How to Use a Journal for Self-guidance and Expanded Creativity** [Paperback] Jeremy P Tarcher Publisher; New Ed edition (1 Dec 1981)